Faith Without Works

Exposing Hidden Agendas And
Revealing The Heart Of God

Kentia R. Middleton

Copyright © 2020 by Kentia R. Middleton

All rights reserved. No part of this publication may be reproduced, distributed or transmitted in any form or by any means, including photocopying, recording, or other electronic or mechanical methods, without the prior written permission of the publisher, except in the case of brief quotations embodied in critical reviews and certain other noncommercial uses permitted by copyright law. For permission requests, write to the publisher, addressed "Attention: Permissions Coordinator," at the address below.

Kentia R. Middleton/Rejoice Essential Publishing
PO BOX 512
Effingham, SC 29541
www.republishing.org

Unless otherwise indicated, scriptures are taken from the King James Version.

Scripture taken from the New King James Version®. Copyright © 1982 by Thomas Nelson. Used by permission. All rights reserved.

Scripture quotations marked "BSB" are taken from The Holy Bible, Berean Study Bible, BSB. Copyright ©2016 by Bible Hub. Used by Permission. All Rights Reserved Worldwide. www.berean.bible

Scripture quotations marked "AMP" are taken from the Amplified® Bible, Copyright © 1954, 1958, 1962, 1964, 1965, 1987 by The Lockman Foundation. Used by permission. www.Lockman.org

The Holy Bible, English Standard Version® (ESV®) Copyright © 2001 by Crossway, a publishing ministry of Good News Publishers. All rights reserved.

Scripture quotations marked (TLB) are taken from The Living Bible copyright © 1971. Used by permission of Tyndale House Publishers, a Division of Tyndale House Ministries, Carol Stream, Illinois 60188. All rights reserved.

Scripture quotations marked (NIV) are taken from the Holy Bible, New International Version®, NIV®. Copyright © 1973, 1978, 1984, 2011 by Biblica, Inc.™ Used by permission of Zondervan. All rights reserved worldwide. www.zondervan.comThe "NIV" and "New International Version" are trademarks registered in the United States Patent and Trademark Office by Biblica, Inc.™

Scripture quotations marked (NLT) are taken from the Holy Bible, New Living Translation, copyright ©1996, 2004, 2015 by Tyndale House Foundation. Used by permission of Tyndale House Publishers, a Division of Tyndale House Ministries, Carol Stream, Illinois 60188. All rights reserved.

Faith Without Works/Kentia R. Middleton
ISBN-13: 978-1-952312-29-8

Library of Congress Control Number: 2020913653

Dedication

I would like to dedicate this book to the Body of Christ. As you read this book, I pray it convicts your heart to seek God and have faith in Him only.

Contents

ACKNOWLEDGMENTS:...................................ix

INTRODUCTION:...1

CHAPTER 1:   Religion............................5

CHAPTER 2:   Witchcraft Prayers:..........10

CHAPTER 3:   Astrology........................14

CHAPTER 4:   Freemasonry, Sororities, and Fraternities......................18

CHAPTER 5:   Sage................................23

CHAPTER 6:   Crystals...........................27

CHAPTER 7:   Yoga and Meditation........31

CHAPTER 8:   Ouija Board.....................36

CHAPTER 9:   Magic..............................40

CHAPTER 10:	Darkness to Light..........46
CHAPTER 11:	The Currency.................67
CHAPTER 12:	Building Your Most Holy Faith.......................74
CHAPTER 13:	Move Mountains..............79
CHAPTER 14:	Faith Journey...................84
CHAPTER 15:	Breaking Generational Curses.............................94
CHAPTER 16:	The Just Shall Live By Faith..........................104
CHAPTER 17:	Faith Without Works....107

ABOUT THE AUTHOR...............................112

REFERENCES.................................115

Acknowledgments

I would like to thank my Lord and Savior Jesus Christ, who has completely changed my life and given me the grace to write this book. I thank Him for downloading the necessary revelation to set the captives free. I would like to thank every organization and person that contributed to my experiences. Without those experiences, I would not be able to write this book. I would like to thank my mentor, Kimberly Moses, for imparting into my life. My life has not been the same since we have connected. I would also like to thank

Tammy Carter for the prophetic word that she gave me, which started my journey to write this book.

Introduction

I was inspired to write this book because I notice the lack of faith in the Body of Christ. I also saw that there are many that say they have faith in God, but they lack works. The Word of God says in James 2:14-26 (NKJV), "What does it profit, my brethren, if someone says he has faith but does not have works? Can faith save him? If a brother or sister is naked and destitute of daily food, and one of you says to them, "Depart in peace, be warmed and filled," but you do not give them the things which are needed for the body, what does it profit? Thus also faith by itself, if it does not have works, is dead. But someone will say, "You have faith, and I have works." Show me your faith without your works, and I will show you my faith by my works. You believe that there is one God. You do well. Even the demons believe—and tremble! But do you want to know, O foolish man, that faith without works is dead? Was not Abraham our father justified by works when he offered Isaac his son on the altar? Do you see that faith was working together with his works, and by works faith was made perfect? And the Scripture was fulfilled which says, "Abraham believed God, and it was accounted to him for righteousness." And he was called the friend of God. You see then that a man is justified by works, and not by faith only. Likewise, was not Rahab the harlot also justified by works when she received the messengers and sent them out another way? For as the body without the spirit is dead, so faith without works is dead also."

Many have confessed Jesus as Lord and Savior, but they continue in witchcraft practices. Mixture has come to the body of Christ. In Revelation 3:15-16 (BSB), "I know your deeds;

you are neither cold nor hot. How I wish you were one or the other! So because you are lukewarm—neither hot nor cold—I am about to vomit you out of My mouth!" So if you confess Jesus but are also dabbling in what He calls impure, you have little faith with no works. Do you really believe the Word of God? If you believed the Word of God, you wouldn't continue in practices that God hates. I am writing this book to open your eyes to the devices of Satan so that you may receive freedom. God wants to give you the opportunity to repent and turn back to His ways and truly believe in Him.

If we truly believe in God and His words in the Bible, the church would look so much different. We have lots of perverse and immoral actions going on in the Body of Christ. God wants us to get back in His will so that the church can go forth in full power and authority. In the first half of this book, I will expose the darkness that has come into the church. Remember, you are the church. The second half of the book will give you the tools to walk in your God given authority in pureness of heart. Through this book, I hope that you will be able to repent from the mixture that has come into your hearts, build your faith by the testimonies, and biblical knowledge and revelation that I write in this book. God bless!

CHAPTER 1

Religion

In the body of Christ, I see this spirit in operation in many churches. This spirit stifles the move of God and holds on to traditions and practices. This spirit quenches the Holy Spirit and the new manifestations that God is trying to release in the lives of His people are blocked. This spirit causes a person to look at the outer appearance of a person and based on their outer appearance, they count them out. Someone can have blue hair and truly have intimacy with God but a person who is under the influence of the religious spirit may rebuke them or condemn them. This spirit brings condemnation and always calls out what is wrong with a person. It is very critical and compares others to themselves. They truly think they are holier than everyone else because they go to church every Sunday since they were a kid. They think they are holier than others because they fast religiously. They are always criticizing others based on the law of the word. This spirit shows no grace. If you mess up once, you are now deemed to hell. They release judgment upon people and there is no redemption in their message.

Many people in the church are under religious leaders. These leaders are influenced by this spirit that's holding back your spiritual growth. You may be growing spiritually, but they tell you that what you are experiencing is not of God. I, unfortunately, dealt with this spirit in 2 churches that I've attended. In the first church, I received words of condemnation and judgment in front of the entire church. I was told that "disease has my name written over it." I was also blamed for making them late because they didn't approve of the outfit that I had on, which belonged to my mother. I went to a store and bought another outfit.

Since we had to make this stop at the store, I was condemned for making them late. At the second church, I was called religious because I spoke to my prophetic mentor's leader because the mentor was using profanity as if it was normal for a Christian leader. As a result of this, I was told I was religious. I was on both sides of the spectrum in these churches. I, both, got to experience religion and then I was called religious.

Many people who go to church do not have a relationship with God. They believe in religion, which is a practice or tradition. They probably never had an encounter with God in their lives. They believe that because they said the sinner's prayer, go to church and listen to the pastor they have a relationship with God. Wrong. There is much more to God than that. We have to get to know Him personally. God desires that we have intimacy with Him and not just rely on religion. Religion will fail you and cause you to never see a breakthrough in your life. Religion will cause you to stay in sin because you need the Spirit of God to bring transformation to your life. I pray that you will understand the importance of having a relationship with God.

We must get free from this spirit because the place that God is taking us, we must be able to flow with the Holy Spirit. God desires that we give up religious practices and truly seek Him with everything that is within us. We have no time to be held back from the places that God is taking us. We have to be able to allow the Holy Spirit to flow in our church services. God didn't call us to ourselves, but He called us to do His work. He has called us so that we may go into all the Earth and preach the gospel. According to Isaiah 61:1-3, "The Spirit of the Lord God is upon me; because the Lord hath anointed me to preach good tidings unto the meek; he hath sent me to bind up the brokenhearted, to proclaim liberty to the captives, and the opening of the prison to them that are bound; To proclaim the acceptable year of the Lord, and the day of vengeance of our God; to comfort all that mourn; To appoint unto them that mourn in Zion, to give unto them beauty for ashes, the oil of joy for mourning, the garment of praise for the spirit of heaviness; that they might be called trees of righteousness, the planting of the Lord, that he might be glorified."

Prayer: Father, I thank You that You are God that delivers. Lord, I'm asking You to deliver me from the spirit of religion. I come out of agreement with this spirit so that your Spirit can be in operation in my life. Father, I ask that You teach me how to be led by your Spirit so that I may walk in everything that You have planned for my life. I thank You that Your plans are of good and not of evil, to give me a future and an expected end according to Jeremiah 29:11. Father, I follow your ways and seek intimacy with You. Teach me how to walk in the Spirit so that I do not fulfill the lust of the flesh. Lord, I do not want to follow the traditions of man, but I want to follow You. Thank You for convicting my heart. Lord, thank You for delivering me in Jesus' name. Amen!

CHAPTER 2

Witchcraft Prayers

Witchcraft is a topic that is rarely discussed, especially in the church. It can be a very touchy topic because it challenges the beliefs and lifestyles of many individuals. There are many practices that people follow because they were passed down from parents, grandparents, and many generations. Does this mean that it is pleasing to God? No. The Bible tells us what is considered witchcraft and that we should not go after

Faith Without Works 11

those practices. Witchcraft comes from the flesh. It operates through fleshly desires of manipulation. When witchcraft is in operation, it does not care who is hurt in the process. Someone is always hurt when witchcraft is being done because someone is under the control of another person against their free will. Many people do not even realize they are operating in witchcraft. Likewise, those that are under control, do not even recognize it. We must make sure that in everything we do, we have the right motives in our hearts and our intentions are to bless and not curse people. We should not want to control someone else's life and destroy it.

God has given us the ability to make our own choices. We can choose what path we want to take in life, whether that be God's path, our own, or the enemy's. He also gave us an avenue to reach Him through prayer. Prayer is a communication method to reach God. Our prayers can be pure or they can be impure. An impure prayer is what I call witchcraft prayers. These are prayers that are out of the will of God. How are we to know we are praying witchcraft prayers? If it does not line up with the will of God (His Word) and against the will of the person you for whom you are praying. Say, for instance, you want someone to be your spouse, but they do not feel the same way or they don't even know you feel this way about them. You begin to pray for them to be your spouse even though you have not consulted God about it or even the person. You are now going against the will of the person and God. Remember in the introduction, I explained that witchcraft is when you are trying to force someone against their own will. It is when you place your desires over theirs and use a certain method to get those desires of yours to manifest. I believe witchcraft prayers are not heard by God but by the devil. He will perform them for you because He wants you to step out of proper alignment with God. We must be very careful not to tap into witchcraft through prayer. When we pray, make sure that it lines up with the will of God. God wants all people to be saved so you may pray for salvation for someone. God wants all people healed and delivered, so it is okay to pray that for someone. When we start going off into "Lord separate this married couple," now we have entered into witchcraft. That goes against the will of God and the will of the married couple.

The Bible says in 1 John 5:14-15, "And this is the confidence that we have in him, that, if we ask anything according to his will, he heareth us: And if we know that he hear us, whatsoever we ask, we know that we have the petitions that we desired of him." The Bible makes it clear that we have to ask according to His will to receive it. We all may have entered into this realm unknowingly, but God wants us to be aware of every area of our lives that will give the enemy a foothold.

Prayer: Father, thank You for Your grace and mercy. I thank You that Your mercy is new every morning. (Lamentations 3:23) Lord, I thank You for revealing my faults to me in love. I thank You that You chastise those You love. (Proverbs 3:12, Hebrews 12:6) Father, thank You for not allowing me to continue in my ignorance. I ask that You forgive me for forcing my will on others through prayer. I thank You that You have shown me right from wrong and I will follow your ways. Thank You for enlightening me in Jesus' name. Amen!

CHAPTER 3

Astrology

What is astrology? Astrology according to Merriam-Webster dictionary, is the divination of the supposed influences of the stars and planets on human affairs and terrestrial events by their position and aspects.1 Astronomy is the science of the stars and planets, but this is trusting the stars and planets to lead your life. Two examples of astrology are horoscopes and zodiac signs.

HOROSCOPES AND ZODIAC SIGNS

I know in society these are things that many people gravitate to in their everyday life. Many people are reading their horoscopes to find direction and guide them for the day. They put their trust in the sun, the stars and the moon to give them clarity on their lives. Many years ago, I used to read my horoscope. I thought that those words were accurate, but now that I am in Christ, I realize that it spoke to my flesh and not my spirit.

Many people gravitate towards their zodiac signs. They think because this describes some of their fleshly attributes it means that they should follow the practice. Zodiac signs are based on the time frame in which you were born. So this practice says that if you were born from this day to that day, you will have these characteristics.

Before I rededicated my life to God, I was claiming my zodiac sign. The characteristics that the zodiac sign said I would have, did match my personality. The revelation I discovered about zodiac signs is it matches my fleshly characteristics. It says that I am a fire sign so I can get angry quickly. When I was in the world, this was true. I was a ticking time bomb. I went from 0 to 100 real quick. The truth of the matter is, for those who have given their lives to Jesus, we are not to conform to this world, but transformed by the renewing of our minds, then we will know what the good, acceptable and perfect will of God is. (Romans 12:2) When we get in the presence of God and read His Word, our character will change and we will no longer act according to the zodiac signs' claims. The Word of God says to walk after the spirit and not the flesh. As I stated before, the zodiac signs represent the characteristics of the flesh.

The Bible clearly tells us that God is a jealous God. Nothing should come before Him. When you claim what your horoscope or zodiac signs say, then you are saying to God that His Word over your life is not true. You are claiming that you are angry and that you will not change because this is what your zodiac sign states. If the Word of God tells us not to go to bed angry, who will we listen to? The Word of God, our horoscope, or our zodiac signs? This is now an idol in our hearts because we are to place no one or thing before God.

Prayer: Father, I thank You for opening my eyes to see the truth. Lord, I repent for coming into agreement with a lie. Lord, your Word clearly tells me who I am and that I should walk in the Spirit and not the flesh. (Galatians 5:16) Lord, I ask that You help me possess the fruit of the spirit, which are love, peace, joy, patience, goodness, kindness, faithfulness, gentleness, and self-control. (Galatians 5:22-23) Lord, teach me how to be led by your Spirit and walk in the good character to which You have called me. Thank You, Lord, for forgiving me and leading me into truth in Jesus' name. Amen!

CHAPTER 4

Freemasonry, Sororities, And Fraternities

I know these are organizations that many people have joined due to family members, and colleges making them seem appealing. Many may not agree with what I say here because to them these groups are "brother/sister" type organizations that bring people together. They do many things for the community. While these things may seem appealing, we have to look at the whole picture and what is behind it all. Anything that does not exalt the name Jesus and Him alone is a cult. These organizations serve other gods. This is what makes it a secret society.

When people join these organizations, they have to do things to get it. They can not tell people about the things that are going on within. Why is it such a secret? What do they have to hide? Why do they have to have an initiation ceremony? Why do they use hand signs? These things are all cultish. Even though it may seem pretty from the outside, what have you really joined? What have you just tied your entire bloodline to?

I do not know much about these organizations since I had never been in one. I do have family members who were and are a part of these organizations. My grandfather was a treasurer in the Freemason and I remember that he wasn't allowed to tell me anything about it. I used to ask him about the secret book that he had and he told me that I could not read it. Well when I rededicated my life to God, these practices came up. When people enter into these organizations, they make covenants with demonic spirits that now attach to the family line. Some of these organizations have the spirit of infirmity, premature death, rebellion, fear, and many more spirits attached to them. You have given these spirits the right to operate in your life and your family. I had to break free from these organizations even though I was not the one who entered into a covenant with them. Before joining these organizations, make sure you understand the consequences that come with them.

As I was led by the Holy Spirit in breaking covenants with the Eastern Stars, I remember reading the 8-page paper and there were some really disturbing consequences for those that wanted to leave these groups. They were basically threatened that they would be fed to the birds if they wanted to detach. I see where the enemy used fear and intimidation tactics to keep people in these organizations. When fear is involved in any group you join, even if it's a church, I need you to reevaluate and really seek God who is in operation. The Word of God says in 1 John 4:18 NKJV, "There is no fear in love; but perfect love casts out fear, because fear involves torment. But he who fears has not been made perfect in love." Now think about it, who is love? God is love. He is that perfect love that drives out fear. So if you have to be bribed into something with fear tactics, you have entered a cult that does not possess the fruits of the spirit: one being love.

There are too many pastors and ministers in the body of Christ in these organizations. If we are supposed to be leading the people of God, but we are dabbling in the occult, how are the people that follow us to be free? We, as leaders, have to make sure we have separated ourselves for the use of God and not desiring to be one with this world. We can not serve two masters. "No man can serve two masters: for either he will hate the one, and love the other; or else he will hold to the one, and despise the other. Ye cannot serve God and mammon." (Matthew 6:24) We need to choose who we will serve. God does not want to share you with anyone else. So today let's make this hard decision even if you have to separate from your "sisters and brothers." Who do you choose this day? "And fear not them which kill the body, but are not able to kill the soul: but rather fear him which is able to destroy both soul and body in hell." (Matthew 10:28)

Prayer: Father, thank You for being God alone. Lord, I thank You that You have opened my eyes to see. Lord, I repent for joining these organizations that do not glorify Your name. Lord, forgive me for my ignorance and help me to walk in Your truth. Lord, help me to separate from these occult practices that are holding me and my family's lives up. Lord, break every evil covenant that I've made in the spirit and allow me and my family to walk free. Lord, break every soul tie that I've made with those that are in these organizations. Lord, I want to be free from everything that is not from You. Thank You for delivering me and giving me a new slate in Jesus' name. Amen!

CHAPTER 5

Sage is an aromatic plant with grayish-green leaves that are used as a culinary herb, native to southern Europe and the Mediterranean.2 Some people use this plant to ward off negative energy by burning it in their homes, which is a Native American tradition. Native Americans worship nature. So my question to you is, why are Christians following this practice or tradition that came from those that worship other gods?

Sage only opens the door for other demonic spirits to come into your home. It may appear that you have peace in your home in the beginning, but I guarantee you that it will get worse. "When an impure spirit comes out of a person, it goes through arid places seeking rest and does not find it. Then it says, 'I will return to the house I left.' When it arrives, it finds the house unoccupied, swept clean and put in order. Then it goes and takes with it seven other spirits more wicked than itself, and they go in and live there. And the final condition of that person is worse than the first. That is how it will be with this wicked generation (Matthew 12:43-45 NIV)."

I've heard stories from people who burned sage to cleanse the atmosphere in their homes and discover that things got worse. This is because they used a substance that is not authorized by God to cleanse the home. We see nowhere in the Bible that the children of God burned sage. We do see in Leviticus 10:1 (NIV), "Aaron's sons Nadab and Abihu took their censers, put fire in them and added incense; and they offered unauthorized fire before the LORD, contrary to his command." So what happened to them? The Bible says in

Leviticus 10:2 (NIV), "So fire came out from the presence of the LORD and consumed them, and they died before the LORD."

We, as the children of God, do not need to use substances that are not biblical to drive out evil spirits. As Christians, we should only use anointing oil, prayer, and laying on of hands to cast out demons. If you have problems with demonic spirits in your home, you need to use the power and authority that Jesus has given you in His name. You should also anoint your home with anointing oil to purify it. "Each day you must sacrifice a young bull as a sin offering to purify them, making them right with the LORD. Afterward, cleanse the altar by purifying it; make it holy by anointing it with oil (Exodus 29:36 NLT)."

Prayer: Father, I realized that I have fallen into error. I repent for not trusting in your power. Lord, forgive me for placing my trust in something other than you to protect me. I know you are a jealous God for your name is Jealous according to Exodus 34:14. I repent for using substances that do not bring glory to Your name. I come out of agreement with these practices and I close all doors to the enemy in Jesus' name. Lord, deliver me from my wrong mindset and teach me through Your Word, so my mind may be renewed. Thank You for a new beginning and fresh start in Jesus' name. Amen!

CHAPTER 6

Crystals

Many Christians have compromised and started using objects such as crystals to receive healing in their mind, body, and soul. These crystals claim to not only have healing properties but are also used for love, reducing stress, bring joy, motivational boost, protection, inner growth, to amplify energy by ridding the mind and body of negative energy and so much more. These practices come from Hinduism and Buddhism. As I was researching this topic, I saw on the same website that they recommend that you burn sage to rid the atmosphere of negative energy too.

Listen, people of God, if you want to do these things, then go all the way with it. Do not mix Christianity with other practices and think that there is nothing wrong with doing it. When you introduce crystals into your life, you are now saying that Jesus dying on the cross was not good enough for you. You are now saying that Isaiah 53:5 holds no weight. "But he was wounded for our transgressions, he was bruised for our iniquities: the chastisement of our peace was upon him, and with his stripes, we are healed (Isaiah 53:5)." I truly believe that many people do not fully follow the commandments of God because they do not want to submit and live holy. If we choose to use crystals, there is no stipulation in place that you have to give something up to receive or whatever it claims to do for you. This is how we can identify that these things are not of God.

I want you to realize that there is power in the name of Jesus. He died, was resurrected, and gained all authority over the enemy. Jesus died so that you may have peace. He is the prince of peace (Isaiah 9:6). He came so that you may have life and that you have it more abundantly (John 10:10). Jesus is more than enough and all you need to receive freedom. Recognize that the enemy wants you to believe these things are working for you but know that everything from him comes with a price. You may feel peace currently but it won't last. The enemy will come to retrieve something from you and if you refuse, that peace will lift and fear will take over your life. The enemy is going to torment your life and you will realize that Jesus is the only one that can give you total peace.

Prayer: Heavenly Father, I thank You for all the revelation you are giving me. Thank You for another chance to get it right. Lord, I repent for using crystals that come against your Word. Lord, forgive me for disregarding Your Son Jesus and the sacrifice He made for mankind. Lord, forgive me for being selfish and trying to take another route to receive peace, healing, protection, joy, and so forth. Lord, I let go of these practices and follow you. Purge me of all unrighteousness and sin and fill me up with your Holy Spirit. Lord, I realize that the Holy Spirit will give me the fruit

I'm searching for according to Galatians 5:22-23. Lord, I turn back to You in Jesus' name. Amen!

CHAPTER 7

Yoga And Meditation

Yoga, according to Merriam-Webster dictionary, is a Hindu theistic philosophy teaching the suppression of all activity of body, mind, and will in order that the self may realize its distinction from them and attain liberation.4 It is a Hindu philosophy that teaches a person to experience inner peace by controlling the body and mind. The definition goes on to say it is a system of physical postures, breathing techniques, and sometimes meditation derived from Yoga, but often practiced independently, especially in Western cultures to promote physical and emotional well-being.

Reading these definitions of the word yoga can cause confusion. They are saying that the capitalized word Yoga is the Hindu religion, while the lowercase word yoga is for exercise. Do not be ignorant of Satan's devices. If you go to yoga class, you will be doing the same movements and meditations that the religion Yoga does. You are channeling the god that they serve and now you have opened your life up for demonic forces to take over. When you meditate during yoga, you are emptying out everything in you but what are you being filled back up with? The Bible says, "When an impure spirit comes out of a person, it goes through arid places seeking rest and does not find it. Then it says, 'I will return to the house I left.' When it arrives, it finds the house unoccupied, swept clean and put in order. Then it goes and takes with it seven other spirits more wicked than itself, and they go in and live there. And the final condition of that person is worse than the first. That is how it will be with this wicked generation (Matthew 12:43-45 NIV)." As you are emptying yourself, you are now inviting evil spirits to come inside of you.

If you read the history of the practice of Hinduism, you would know that they have a guru. This is a spiritual guide, a person who teaches others how to practice. They meditate a lot and empty themselves so that spirits may channel through them. I was watching "Sid Roth: It's Supernatural" one day, and he interviews a guy who used to be a guru. He emptied himself out so much through meditation that these spirits took over his body. He was able to heal bodies and such, but if the person did not stay connected to him or in a certain mile radius, their healing would reverse. He said he would feel the spirit come through his feet. He was not able to speak anymore either. I am saying all of this because this ex-guru practiced yoga and meditation and was possessed by those spirits. He was no longer in control of his body.

As believers in Jesus Christ, we must not participate in every doctrine or practice. "That we henceforth be no more children, tossed to and fro, and carried about with every wind of doctrine, by the sleight of men, and cunning craftiness, whereby they lie in wait to deceive (Ephesians 4:14)." We need to make sure that what we are doing does not come against the Word of God. Just because the dictionary tries to separate the two, does not mean that in the spiritual realm it is separated. The only spirit that we want to be in us is the Holy Spirit because it is the Spirit of God. We are carrying the very presence of God each day that will lead and guide us into all things that are true. We will not be led wrong or fall into deception.

According to the Word of God, we should meditate on His Word day and night (Joshua 1:8). When we meditate on the Word of God, it gets in our hearts (mind) and we are able to stand on His Word no matter the circumstance. People use yoga to clear their minds and for peace, but the only way they will receive what they are looking for is in the Word of God. The Bible says that Jesus is the prince of peace (Isaiah 9:6). So receive your peace today in Jesus' name.

Faith Without Works

Prayer: Father, thank You for always giving us a chance to be redeemed. Thank You for Your Son Jesus and that He died for my sins. Lord, I repent for opening doors to the enemy by meditating and doing yoga. Lord, forgive me for my lack of knowledge. Your Word says we should meditate on Your Word day and night according to Joshua 1:8. Lord, as I meditate on Your Word you are filling me up with more of you. I let go of these practices that came from other gods. Lord, I only want to glorify Your name. I pray that you continue to enlighten me and lead me by your Spirit in Jesus' name. Amen!

CHAPTER 8

Ouija Board

An Ouija board is a device consisting of a small board, or planchette, on legs that rest on a larger board marked with words, letters of the alphabet, etc., and that by moving over the larger board and touching the words, letters, etc., while the fingers of spiritualists, mediums, or others rest lightly upon it, is employed to answer questions, give messages, etc.5 This definition clearly shows that mediums and spiritualists use this to receive answers. As children of God, we are neither of these. We do not channel spirits or conjure any of them up because we have the Holy Spirit, the Spirit of God living on the inside of us.

This board is usually used in our society by children and teenagers. They have these in stores as board games. They make it seem so innocent by placing it in the board game section so that your children would be drawn to it. Little do parents know, they are opening their children's lives and possibly homes to demonic forces. Many people have been tormented in their homes after using ouija boards because they did not realize they were really tapping into the spiritual realm illegally.

There was a news story going around where some people made a huge ouija board because they wanted to conjure up really big spirits. These people are ignorant and blinded by the enemy. The enemy wants to use them to bring more demonic spirits into the Earth. They might think that this is a game and they are just having fun, but they are actually inviting these demonic spirits into their lives and their children's lives for 3 to 4 generations. "The LORD is slow to anger and abounding in steadfast love, forgiving iniquity and transgression, but he will by no means clear the guilty, visiting the iniquity of the fathers on the children, to the third and the fourth generation (Numbers 14:18 ESV)." They are creating a generational curse because they are opening the door to the enemy. They have literally invited him into their world and said "have your way." God does not want us to be ignorant of Satan's devices. He is opening our eyes now so that we may walk in total deliverance and victory for ourselves and our family members. If you have one of these boards, I suggest that you burn it and ask God to forgive you for stepping into territories that opened up doors to the enemy.

Prayer: Father, I lift Your Son's name today. Father, I repent for doing things that are an abomination to You. Lord, I turn from my wicked ways and turn back to Your Son Jesus. Lord, You are the only help I know. Father, I close all demonic doors in my life that I've opened from using ouija boards. Father, cleanse me and protect me from all harm and danger I have brought upon myself. I thank You that You are forgiving and merciful to those that repent and turn back to You. Lord, turn my stony heart to a heart of flesh so I may receive only You. I thank You for grace and mercy in Your Son Jesus' name. Amen!

CHAPTER 9

Magic

According to Merriam-Webster dictionary, magic is the use of means (such as charms or spells) believed to have supernatural power over natural forces.6 Magic is not a hidden form of witchcraft like some of the other practices in our society. It is used to manipulate natural elements such as the mind, the body, the weather, and much more. This is not unto God, but the power comes from darkness.

flesh so I may receive only You. I thank You for grace and mercy in Your Son Jesus' name. Amen!

CHAPTER 9

Magic

According to Merriam-Webster dictionary, magic is the use of means (such as charms or spells) believed to have supernatural power over natural forces.6 Magic is not a hidden form of witchcraft like some of the other practices in our society. It is used to manipulate natural elements such as the mind, the body, the weather, and much more. This is not unto God, but the power comes from darkness.

WHITE MAGIC

Throughout my life, I've heard people talk about being a good witch. They use white magic because they claim that they are not doing it to harm anyone. This type of magic still manipulates a person, so there is no good in it. The person they are using it on does not know they are being controlled, which makes it witchcraft.

The title "Christian witch" that is used in our society uses this form of witchcraft. If the Bible speaks against witches, why do we think in our society that it is acceptable to God? The Bible says in Exodus 22:18, Thou shalt not suffer a witch to live. Back in these days, those who were witches would be stoned because they came against the true and living God. Jesus came to redeem mankind, so this is no longer the case. God is not pleased with the works of those that do white magic. He wants to redeem you from operating in practices that come against His plan for your life and those you manipulate with magic. He is calling you to repent and come into the knowledge of the true and living God. He created you for a purpose and He has a plan for your life.

His plan is not of evil but of good, to give you a future and a hope (Jeremiah 29:11). There is a future for you in God and it does not involve you dabbling in witchcraft or mixing Christianity with magic.

BLACK MAGIC

When I looked up the definition of black magic in Merriam-Webster dictionary, it said that it is magic associated with the devil or evil spirits: evil magic.7 This type of magic is used to bring harm to people. While some may use white magic for protection, this type of magic is used to steal, kill, and destroy your life. There are so many occult practices but I will group many of them under black magic; Santeria, roots, psychics, juju, voodoo, new age, and much more. None of these practices glorify God. If you say that you are a Christian but you are going to see a witch, a wizard, obeah, shaman, etc. repent now. Turn from these practices and turn back to the only true and living God. The things that these people offer are bringing you and your family into more bondage each time. Remember, the enemy requires something from you; nothing is free. "Regard not them that have familiar spirits, neither seek after wizards, to be defiled by them: I [am] the LORD your God (Leviticus 19:31)." "When thou art come into the land which the LORD thy God giveth thee, thou shalt not learn to do after the abominations of those nations. There shall not be found among you [any one] that maketh his son or his daughter to pass through the fire, [or] that useth divination, [or] an observer of times, or an enchanter, or a witch, Or a charmer, or a consulter with familiar spirits, or a wizard, or a necromancer. For all that do these things [are] an abomination unto the LORD: and because of these abominations the LORD thy God doth drive them out from before thee (Deuteronomy 18:9-12)."

God does not want His people to be ignorant and stay in the same cycles for the rest of their lives. He wants to open your eyes so you may know the truth to get set free. "Idolatry, witchcraft, hatred, variance, emulations, wrath, strife, seditions, heresies, envyings, murders, drunkenness, revellings, and such like: of the which I tell you before, as I have also told [you] in time past, that they which do such things shall not inherit the kingdom of God (Galatians 5:20-21)." The Word of God already tells you that the Kingdom of God won't be yours if you partake in these practices. God wants His people to have pure hearts and to seek Him for everything they need. God has everything you need within Him and you do not need to seek darkness to receive protection or revenge for something someone has done to you. You do not need to manipulate anyone's life to make it fit with yours. You are not God and you do not want the judgment of God to fall upon you for the wickedness of your heart. Today repent in the name of Jesus. Renounce these practices and come back to Your first love. God is the only one that can save you, deliver you, love you, give you peace, joy, and happiness. Let go of falsehood today!

Prayer: Dear Heavenly Father,

I thank You that You have opened my eyes to the truth. I thank You for being a forgiving God and giving me the opportunity to get it right with you. Lord, I repent for having idols in my heart and using dark practices to manipulate the lives of others. Lord, I know You are not pleased with my choices, and this day I chose to let go of everything that grieves You. Lord, I repent for not trusting You to deliver me and avenge me from things that have caused harm and hurt in my life. Forgive me Lord for all the lives I've destroyed and for coming against Your plan for their lives. Lord, forgive me for seeking counsel from everything but You. Lord, forgive me for not trusting You with my life. Lord, I want to get to know You and understand Your will for my life. I know You have a plan for me according to Jeremiah 29:11. I thank You for forgiving me and setting me free in Jesus' name. Amen!

CHAPTER 10

Darkness To Light

Now that I have exposed the dark practices that are holding the body of Christ captive, I will take you on a journey revealing the heart of God for your life. God wants you to believe that His word is spirit and life (John 6:63). His Word is active and alive according to Hebrew 4:12. "For the word of God is living and active, sharper than any two-edged sword, piercing to the division of soul and of spirit, of joints and of marrow, and discerning the thoughts and intentions of the heart. And no creature is hidden from his sight, but all are naked and exposed to the eyes of him to whom we must give account (Hebrew 4:12-13)." God wants us to realize that His Word has enough power and authority to change a situation. We do not have to dabble in wicked practices to receive power and authority. Many people do not have the patience or possess the fruits of the Holy Spirit. "But the fruit of the Spirit is love, joy, peace, patience, kindness, goodness, faithfulness, gentleness, and self-control. There is no law against things like this (Galatians 5:22-23 CEB)." When we truly surrender to God and His will and let go of these demonic practices, we will see the Word of God break the barriers that have been holding our breakthroughs.

God wants to bless His people so that we may possess the land and territories that are hindered and stolen by the enemy. He wants His people to walk in power and authority that we were given when Jesus died and rose in full power. We serve a God that is more than enough. He is more than we could ever ask or imagine. "Now to Him who is able to do exceedingly abundantly above all that we ask or think, according to the power that works in us, to Him be glory in the church by Christ Jesus to all generations, forever and ever. Amen (Ephesians 3:20-21)." God wants to work through us but our wells must be pure. Pure water has to flow out of us with no tainted beliefs and practices. I believe as you continue to read this book, you will receive the revelation you need to build your faith and purge wrong mindsets so that your well may be pure.

I will share my experiences with witchcraft in the church so that you may learn to test every spirit. "Beloved, believe not every spirit, but try the spirits whether they are of God: because many false prophets are gone out into the world (1 John 4:1)."

WITCHCRAFT IN THE CHURCH

I shared my testimony in my first book, More Than Enough: Rejected by Man but Accepted by God, but I didn't tell the whole story. Since then I've received more revelation on what took place. I started going to a church in 2017 after being invited by a coworker. She was going to this church for about a year at the time and thought it was a good idea that I came. I attended church the first time with my husband on December 24, 2017. I had a great experience being that my husband and I received prayer and I got a prophetic word that was confirmation to what God was speaking to me already. This church was very different from any I had attended in my youth because it was multicultural. My pastors were Caucasian and the church was filled with many nationalities. I did not attend church regularly in the beginning because the church was about 45 minutes away from my house. Every time I went to church, someone would prophesy to me and it helped me see my future and not the situation I was in.

As I continued to go to this church, I realized something was missing. I had been in church as a teenager and I encountered the presence of God every church service. At this church, I had very few encounters with the presence of God after going there for two years. I would ask God during service, "Where are you?" I mentioned to you that I received prophetic words but as I received them, there was no fire on the word. I did sense the presence of God on some people as they sang or prophesied.

In January 2019, I decided to pursue leadership development. This church believes in the fivefold ministry. They train and equip those that are called to those offices. So every Wednesday, I started going to leadership development. They tried to put me in the pastor's development groups when I knew that God called me a prophet. So I had to go to the pastor to get that straightened out. As I went to these classes, the gift of discerning of spirits started kicking in strong. I didn't have these experiences that I will be discussing below until I was placed in prophetic development.

I had a dream that I was walking down a road. As I kept walking, I ended up at a stadium that was located by the water. There were rocks and water coming in on the shore. There were people standing down by the water and I was sitting in the stadium. Suddenly, a woman (in the dream I knew she was the leader) got a big demonic mask and put it up to her face. I said, "Wait, what are you doing?" She said, "I'm about to conjure up some spirits." I said, "I will serve the true and living God and Him only." I got my two children and left. I started walking back down the road and I looked at my cell phone. It was at 23%. This was the first dream I had but it did not stop here. I believe God was trying to warn me of the practices of the leaders.

At this church, you had to go through certain training to be able to pray and prophesy at the altar. There was this one woman who I know for a fact was only going to this church for a few months, but she was up there praying for people. Every time I went up to an altar call and got her or another specific woman praying for me, I would have demonic dreams that night. I would have sexual dreams every time they laid hands on me. I also had a dream of the first woman I mentioned standing on a stage with many people in the audience. She was on the stage with her fiancé. She started talking about God when someone in the audience interrupted and said that they did not want to hear from people committing fornication. This dream could have represented my thought about her, or it could have been God telling me why I was having these dreams after receiving prayer from her.

In April, I had a dream that I shared with the head prophetess of this church and she said she believed God was calling me to the prophetic. She asked if I would like to be the receptionist to a prophetic team that she had put together between services. People were able to make appointments and receive prophetic ministry every other Sunday. So now I'm the receptionist of this prophetic team and my job is to make everyone coming in for prophetic ministry comfortable and hold a conversation until they're ready to go into their session. I started receiving prophetic words for those people as I held conversations and the head prophetess heard one day as she came to check on us and asked if I wanted to be on the prophetic team. I agreed. She also assigned me a prophetic mentor so that she could monitor the words I give.

I was placed on teams with two other prophets. I enjoyed doing this because the people were blessed by the prophetic words. Around this time, I started meeting up with the mentor. She offered me a job because I did not work since God told me to quit my job the year before. I took a course at this church called "School of the Prophets," where they used my birthdate to prophesy my destiny. They said I was a prayer warrior, intercessor, priest, pastoral anointing, prophetic, and have the spirit of counsel all from my birthdate and year. I didn't know how biblical this was but they said the Bible has a whole book called Numbers. So based on the fact that I was told I had the spirit of counsel, I decided to go to school for professional counseling after they agreed too.

When I met with the mentor to discuss my prophetic journey and the new job I would be starting, she started using profanity. I thought I was tripping the first time, but she kept talking and used more profanity. I didn't know what to think of it, so I brushed it off. She was my boss on the job so sometimes she would work with me. As we were working together, she started using profanity there. I was so disturbed. I started praying for her every day and asking God to reveal her faults to her. Nothing was changing. Over time the Holy Spirit in me was so grieved. I had the fear of man so I ended up telling the head prophet that assigned this mentor to me. She called me and basically called me religious without saying it directly. She was defending the mentor as if using profanity was normal. This was a deal-breaker for me because I know that as a prophet, God deals with the mouth first. "So I said: "Woe is me, for I am undone! Because I am a man of unclean lips, And I dwell in the midst of a people of unclean lips; For my eyes have seen the King, The Lord of hosts." Then one of the seraphim flew to me, having in his hand a live coal which he had taken with the tongs from the altar. And he touched my mouth with it, and said: "Behold, this has touched your lips; Your iniquity is taken away, And your sin purged (Isaiah 6:5-7 NKJV)."

Now I knew for sure I was in the midst of false prophets. I sent them bible Scriptures to back up my reasoning for the things I said. I told them that I did not think it was good for her to mentor others because if she was mentoring someone who had issues with using profanity, they would think it's okay or fall back into doing that if they were trying to stop. Nothing I said was being received by them. I was about to leave the church at this point because we obviously had different

Faith Without Works 55

beliefs, morals, and standards. I did not want to associate myself with those that call clean unclean and vice versa.

This was a pretty big church, so we were assigned to pastors that were under the head pastors. Well, one of my pastors texted me and asked if everything was okay. I never told her what was going on prior to her contacting me and that I was contemplating leaving. She told me to talk to one of the head pastors (husband and wife) at the church first because she would assure me that this was not what they believed. I met up with the pastor that seems to handle everything at the church and she is the one I see everyone going to all the time. She told me she talked to the mentor and the head prophetess about the situation. She also agreed with me but gave me biblical knowledge of how I should have handled it by going to the mentor first. Then she asked if I was still leaving. Since she seemed to have standards, I decided to stay, but I mentioned to her that I was no longer comfortable being on the prophetic team. She suggested that I talk to the mentor and discuss any issues that I may have had. I met up with her one day and we discussed what was bothering me. Even though some shade was thrown at me, I just forgot about it and decided to proceed forward with no hard feelings. When I went to church one day, the prophetess came up to me and hugged me and asked if I could do the prophetic team again. I agreed.

During this time, I was already under attack. The attacks started in April when I started on the prophetic team and when I was assigned to this mentor. My legs and feet were going numb all the time. One day I went to the altar to receive prayer because of this. When I left the church, I was walking to my husband's truck. My legs wouldn't move. He had to drive up to me and I had to pull myself inside. This was the beginning of much more warfare to come. Not only was my leg going numb as I walked, but I started having brain fog. One day at work, I stood in one section for hours because I could not think of what to do. My mind was so foggy. It didn't stop there. My eyes stopped focusing. When I looked at things, I could not focus on it. My eyes were blurry even though I had my glasses on. I would ask for prayer at church for this at the altar, from my pastors, and received no relief. Since this was happening to me, I had to quit school because I could not see nor focus on reading the material for the classes I was taking. I also quit the job because I could not focus on doing the work, my legs kept going numb and I wasn't able to walk at times. There was so much warfare. I ended up going to the hospital and they said my blood sugar was 485. I was already healed by God from diabetes, so I didn't know why this had reoccurred.

I was also attacked in my room for two mornings. My husband went to work and I decided to sleep in his spot. The first time, I fell asleep and woke up in a dream in my bed. I was laying with the covers over my head. I felt a presence enter my room. All of a sudden, something jumped on me and the bed was shaking vigorously. The second time, the same thing happened. I went to sleep and woke up in a dream in my bed. The covers were over my head again. It reminded me of the last experience I had, so I was aware and not going to let that happen again. I kicked my feet and someone fell over. When I woke up, my feet were still kicking. I mentioned this to the mentor and she said, "Good thing you were able to defend yourself." I was also being told by the leaders at this church that the dreams I was having were not from God. They would say, "Why would God show you that?" Or they would make me think that God was showing me a person's past and not what they are currently struggling with.

I continued to press through all the warfare. The woman who introduced me to this church called me one day concerned. She said she was going through a lot of warfare. She was seeing many demonic images, such as her fingers being cut off. We decided to meet up and discuss what we had been discerning. She had stopped going to church for a month and the warfare stopped for her. She had seen other wicked things going on that made her not want to go back. We prayed together and knew that God was not pleased with the leadership at the church. There were many hidden things, but God started revealing them to us. I had a dream about a prophet at the church. I was on the phone with her and in the dream, I knew she was a witch. In reality, she had recently tattooed a dragon on her hand. She had also been drawing and doing artwork of dragons. I remember prophesying to her in one of these prophetic sessions because she was confused about whether she was hearing from God or not. The pastor had gotten on her about that dragon tattoo she had gotten. She was over the youth at the church.

On September 1, 2019, I started a blog after feeling led by God to do so. I went to church for leadership development the day before all hell broke loose in my life. The same woman who would pray for me and I would have the demonic dreams spoke to me. She said she liked my blog and was proud of me but... I was like "but what?" She was beating around the bush to tell me what she wanted to say. She basically said I wasn't using proper English and that she was an English major. As she was talking, I discerned that she was jealous. At the end of the night, another woman ran up to me as I was leaving to go home. She started talking to me about a journey we both were on at the church. She then grabbed my hands and started praying for me. I thought it was pretty weird but I proceeded to let her and went home. The next day on September 12, 2019, I was under a witchcraft attack. This was added to what was already going on before. I was sitting in my room, talking to my mom on the phone when all of a sudden, my body got stiff, my tongue was stiff, I couldn't talk, and I could barely breathe. This lasted for about 20 to 30 seconds maybe. I could hear my mom saying, "Hello, Ken, you there." I immediately contacted some intercessors that did not attend my church and they prayed for me. One person discerned it was witchcraft right away. Well later on that day, it happened again. I didn't know what to do. This was the beginning of a 21-day journey of pure torment. The next day, it got more intense and more frequent. I ended up calling the EMS because I thought I was having seizures or strokes. I was taken to the hospital. They could not find anything wrong with me. As days went on, it got more intense. I could not move without this stroke type situation happening to me. I talked to the administrator of the church and asked to get some anointing oil because of what was going on. She told me to come and get it. My daughter took me along with my sister and son. As soon as we pulled into the churchyard, I had an episode. The pastor came to the car with the administrator and prayed a quick prayer. I still had no relief as I left the church going into more episodes.

Faith Without Works

I was still in contact with my church and they said they were praying for me. I received no relief. The mentor told me to call someone that was connected to our church but not a member. As soon as I spoke to this woman, she said "Who have you been around doing witchcraft?" I told her the only places I went to was to church and home. She said, "Who does the pastor have praying there?" She asked who was praying for me there and I told her but she wasn't familiar with the names. She was praying for me daily. One of my sessions with her over the phone, she said she saw a huge snake with a wolf's head come off of my head as she prayed. It tried to lash at her, but she said the Holy Spirit told her to scream in its mouth and when she did it broke apart. I immediately felt weak. So weak, I thought I was going to die. She said it might have been the spirit that attacked me in my room prior. I do not know but I believe it was a witch that had astral projected.

At this point, I was unable to take care of my children, so my mom came to stay with me. I was basically handicap. I needed someone to take me to the bathroom, wash me up, fix my food, change my clothes, and tend to my son. I needed someone to be with me at all times because these episodes would happen as I made any little movement. I was growing weary, but I was not going to give up. I went to this church one last time with my mom, daughter, and son. One of my pastors was going to meet me to help me inside. She got me in the church after I had an episode getting out of the car and she asked some leaders that were standing around to pray for me. They started prophesying open doors and everything that I did not want to hear. I needed someone to go to war by praying warfare prayers to break the attack. After they prophesied, I went into the church to sit down, got through service, went to the altar, and still was having these episodes in front of everyone. One prophet came up to me and said she never saw me this way. She tried to encourage me to get up and don't let whatever was going on to keep me down. She had no idea what was going on. Everyone was leaving the church but no one had stopped to help me. I saw the pastor and head prophet look at me and leave. I was heartbroken at this point. This was my last time going to this church. My family burned everything I had ever received from this church.

I needed answers as to what was going on. I went into deep prayer one morning and the Lord revealed three of the sources. He showed me a woman's face, I heard Santeria and I saw a python snake. Now I knew what was happening. I was feeling this python wrap around me and squeezing the breath out of me, but for some reason, I could feel it in the natural. I was starting to get so weak spiritually. Life was being sucked out of me. I continued in warfare prayer in my house. I would walk up and down the house speaking in tongues loudly. I heard my tongues shift into warfare tongues. The episodes would still happen as I went into warfare, but I was not going to back down. I was fighting for my freedom. I was still being attacked by the spirit of Jezebel as well. I was having all types of demonic visions and dreams. I had dreams that I was being accused of things I hadn't done. I also was having dreams of people shooting at me. One night I had another dream that confirmed the python spirit. I dreamed that I was in the basement of some pastors' house that I had been watching recently (husband and wife). There were many old washing machines and dryers all around. They were old and rusty. One new set was sitting in the middle of the floor. All of a sudden, a yellow python snake was coming up to my son and me. I grabbed him and the snake went under a table. I grabbed something to go after it and kill it but I couldn't find it and woke up. I believe this dream revealed to me the hidden agenda and life of my pastors. My son and I were the only ones in my household actively going to this church.

One day at the end of September, I received victory over the python spirit. I was speaking in tongues warring in the spirit. It tried to squeeze me but I continued speaking in tongues no matter how hard it was for me to breathe or speak. I placed my hands on my right arm (where I felt the attack) and I continued speaking in tongues even though my tongue was stiffening up and I was slurring. It broke. I felt that python die. It was such a relief. This was not the end of my battle though. I was dealing with the spirit of fear now. It tried to masquerade as the python spirit but I could discern that it wasn't the same spirit. I could breathe now when the episodes would happen and I did not feel the squeezing effect. Around this same time, I got counsel from a true prophet that helped me to become free from everything. She saw a witch blowing black smoke on me in the spirit. I followed her advice and the attacks stopped. The spirit of fear kept coming back trying to get me to agree with it, but I kept using the Word of God against it and binding it up in Jesus' name.

I wrote this section because I want everyone to be careful with who they connect. Just because someone calls themselves a prophet does not make them a prophet of God. Just because people serve in the church, does not mean they are living holy. Be careful what church you attend because there are many cults and religious organizations imitating Holy Spirit-filled churches. Test the spirit and never doubt what God is showing you about those around you. I went through all of these demonic attacks because I was connected to witches and warlocks masquerading as prophets. "Beware of false prophets, which come to you in sheep's clothing, but inwardly they are ravening wolves (Matthew 7:15)." The Holy Spirit gave me this revelation about them after all the smoke was cleared. Many people operate from the gift and not because they are anointed. Gifts and callings are without repentance (Romans

11:29). Someone could be called by God but they step into another realm due to disobedience. The Bible also gives us an example in Acts 16:16, how someone can operate from the spirit of divination (python) and be accurate. In the next chapter, I will take you on a journey that will help you on your faith walk.

CHAPTER 11

The Currency

Faith is the currency in the Kingdom of Heaven, as money is the currency in the Earth. We must have faith that what we are praying for according to the will of God is being produced in the Spirit. We have to believe that those things that are being produced in the spirit, will manifest in the Earth. We should be kingdom-minded, keeping our minds on the things above and not beneath. "Set your minds on things above, not on earthly things (Colossians 3:2 NIV)." Our help comes from above, so no matter what is going on in our lives, we have to keep our faith in Christ. "But without faith it is impossible to please him: for he that cometh to God must believe that he is, and that he is a rewarder of them that diligently seek him (Hebrew 11:6)."

To get the attention of God, we must have childlike faith. And he said: "Truly I tell you, unless you change and become like little children, you will never enter the kingdom of heaven (Matthew 18:3)." If we keep the mindset of an adult who is mature and may think we know it all based on our experience, we won't be able to receive from God. God wants us to put down everything that we know and or may have been taught to seek His face. In His face, we will learn of His ways, His character, His desires, and His plan. Then we will be able to go forth in Him and know for sure that He has told us to do those things.

I love to look at my son to learn childlike faith. My son does not question me when I tell him to do something. He trusts that what I'm telling Him will not hurt him or lead him the wrong way. This is the same way we should be looking at our Heavenly Father when He tells us to do things.

Faith Without Works

Remember that He will never lead us wrong. He wants us to trust Him and grow from the direction that He gives us. Remember, He knows our future because He planned it out before the foundations of the Earth. There is nothing wrong with asking God questions because He wants us to seek Him out to find out what He has revealed to us. How else are we to know what He wants? I remember growing up hearing my grandmother say, "Do not question God." I never understood her logic because if I don't understand, how else am I to receive the answer? The Word of God tells us in Matthew 7:7-8, "Ask, and it shall be given you; seek, and ye shall find; knock, and it shall be opened unto you: For everyone that asketh receiveth; and he that seeketh findeth; and to him that knocketh it shall be opened." God wants to reveal Himself more and more to us, but we must have faith to believe that He will.

The Bible tells us that Noah had faith when God told him to build an ark even though it looked crazy to others. God may tell us to do things that seem weird or out of the norm, but we have to trust in God. When I quit my job, some people thought I was out of my mind. They would say,

"You shouldn't quit your job until you've found another one." I knew what God had told me and it wasn't to worry about another job. He did say He has greater elsewhere but that doesn't even mean it's another job. See, we have to stop letting people influence us to disobey God with our Earthly wisdom and receive the wisdom that comes from God. The Bible says that God uses the foolish things to confound the wise (1 Corinthians 1:27). What we deem as foolish, God will use that same thing to get His point across.

I was guilty of letting people influence me to disobey God by following their instructions. On May 13, 2019, I did two things that God did not tell me to do. Actually, He gave me a dream on April 1, 2019, where He showed me that I was pregnant in the spirit. I was supposed to get induced at 4 pm according to the nurse in the dream. I fell asleep and missed my appointment. I woke up at 5:13 pm looking for the nurse. I was not able to find her. The Lord was trying to warn me not to take the opportunities that would arise on 5/13 because I would miss Him. Instead, I took the advice of some leaders at my church after revealing this dream to them. "So that your faith might not rest in the wisdom of men but in the power of God (1 Corinthians 2:5 ESV)." They offered me a job and thought it was a good idea to go to school for counseling. Ironically both the job and school started on 5/13. None of these things were the will of God for my life and I quickly learned of that as I tried to walk them out. These things didn't last two months as I was attacked spiritually by demonic forces. My lack of faith in what God showed me cost me and induced unnecessary warfare.

In Hebrews 11, it talks about the faith of Abraham. He left behind everything and went out into foreign territories following the Word of the Lord about his inheritance. He didn't think twice or question the Lord, he had childlike faith and believed God no matter what the circumstances may have looked like. Even though Abraham and his wife were well past childbearing age, they still believed that God would provide. There were times that their faith was tested. Sarah was impatient and lacked faith in the promise of God. She convinced her husband that he should conceive a baby with her maid. Once the child came, Sarah became jealous and no longer wanted the maid nor the son of her husband to stay with them. This is a perfect example of why we should not do things on our own but wait on the Lord because He has the perfect timing for all things to manifest. Following our own ways and thinking we know it all can cause unnecessary events from taking place in our lives. They ultimately did receive the promise of God many years later.

Peter had faith to step onto the water with Jesus but allowed the distraction of the wind to cause him to sink (Matthew 14:28-31). Many times we step out in faith and start off good. We see the clear path set before us but as soon as an issue appears, we start to sink. We allow people, the enemy, time, circumstances to distract us from where God is trying to take us. We must have the faith as Peter did, but we must keep our eyes on Jesus and allow nothing to shake us and cause us to sink. Reading the book of Acts shows great progress in Peter's faith. We see him moving powerfully with authority and great faith. Peter's faith became so strong in God that his shadow healed the sick (Acts 5:15).

From my personal experiences and biblical stories, I want you to see that even though God places the perfect plan before us, we often fail by doing things our own way. God is a merciful God and He allows us to venture on other paths to teach us a lesson. When we exit those tests, we are now much wiser and are able to grow in God because of the lessons learned. We also learn that the way of the Lord is sure and we do not have to operate in our own strength. God knows what He is doing and He knows the way that we would take. "But He knows the way that I take; When He has tested me, I shall come forth as gold (Job 23:10 NKJV)." Just know that every mistake or success is to take you to your next level of faith. We go from faith to faith and glory to glory as we allow the Holy Spirit to bring transformation to our lives. "For in it the righteousness of God is revealed from faith for faith, as it is written, "The righteous shall live by faith (Romans 1:17 ESV)."

CHAPTER 12

Building Your Most Holy Faith

The Word of God tells us in Jude 1:20, "But ye, beloved, building up yourselves on your most holy faith, praying in the Holy Ghost," If you lack faith in God because you are facing a hard trial, I challenge you to pray in the Holy Ghost (Holy Spirit). If you have not yet received the gift of speaking in tongues, ask God. He says that He gives good gifts to His children. "Which of you, if his son asks for bread, will give him a stone? Or if he asks for a fish, will give him a snake? So if you who are evil know how to give good gifts to your children, how much more will your Father in heaven give good things to those who ask Him (Matthew 7:9-11 BSB)!" God wants you to speak in tongues so that you would be able to communicate in your Heavenly language orchestrated by the Holy Spirit. The Holy Spirit will lead and guide you into all things that are true. So when you speak in tongues, your faith will be increased in God because the Holy Spirit is praying through you. The perfect will of God is being prayed back to God. You will start to see your faith rise because many prayers that you have been petitioning in your natural language are now being spoken in your Heavenly language. Whatever it is that God has planned out for your life will begin to manifest. This is why praying in tongues will build your faith. The things that you are hoping for that you do not see will begin to manifest.

My life changed drastically when I started speaking in tongues. I received this revelation from my mentor when I took her class "School of the Prophets." After this, I also encountered an angel in my dream that laid next to me and told me to speak in tongues loudly for at least one hour per day. In that dream, I repeated the Scripture Jude 1:20 back to him. I started speaking in tongues daily for at least an hour for about two years now. My life has really changed. I used to be stuck in a place and didn't see my way out. As I continued to speak in tongues daily, building up my most holy faith, the Lord started giving me direction for my life. He started revealing to me the areas I needed to make changes and which areas I was on the right track. Many of you are stuck and do not know what God is requiring of you. I tell you, follow this Jude 1:20 principle and your life will begin to shift.

If we look at the life of Paul, he said in 1 Corinthians 14:18 that he speaks in tongues more than us all. He wrote most of the new testament. How did he receive so much revelation? Speaking in tongues allowed him to know the heart and mind of God to be able to lead each church that he went to. He was full of the power and authority of Jesus Christ. His faith was built so strong because he was always praying in tongues.

God desires that we embrace the Holy Spirit. The Holy Spirit is our helper, our counselor, and much more. But the Helper (Comforter, Advocate, Intercessor—Counselor, Strengthener, Standby), the Holy Spirit, whom the Father will send in My name [in My place, to represent Me and act on My behalf], He will teach you all things. And He will help you remember everything that I have told you. (John 14:26 AMP) When we invite the Holy Spirit into our lives, we will be strengthened in our walk with God and receive counsel straight from the throne of grace. In a chapter below, I will tell you about my experience when God told me to quit my job. I stepped out in faith even though I could not see ahead of me, but I trusted that God was telling me the truth. After I did what God told me to do, I went on a journey with the Holy Spirit and He started showing me many things that have taken me to the place I am currently today. I started a blog on September 1, 2019, called 'More Than Enough'. The Lord directed me to share my testimony and He gives me prophetic messages and words of encouragement. I published my first book called More Than Enough: Rejected by Man but Accepted by God in January 2020. I started my ministry called Freedom in Christ Deliverance Ministries in April 2020. I also launched my first business in April of 2020 called KRM Creative Designs. I tell you all of this to say that when you pray in your most holy faith, your faith in God increases, you receive direction for your life, you come out of stuck places, and you begin to walk in purpose and destiny.

CHAPTER 13

Move Mountains

Do you know that faith can move mountains? Matthew 17:20 NLT says, "You don't have enough faith," Jesus told them. "I tell you the truth, if you had faith even as small as a mustard seed, you could say to this mountain, 'Move from here to there,' and it would move. Nothing would be impossible." Jesus was telling his disciples that they only needed small faith. A mustard seed is a very small seed measuring at about 0.039 to 0.079 inches in diameter. It amazes me that if we have faith that small, we can move a mountain. Wow, so any situation or circumstance that we may be facing, we can move it with such little faith. Even though we may not see anything happening, when we speak to that mountain, it has no choice but to move. When we have faith, nothing will be impossible for us. If we are currently facing sickness in our bodies, we can speak to that mountain and it has to move. That mountain has to go because the Word of God says by the stripes of Jesus, we are healed (Isaiah 53:5).

James 1:6 (NIV) says, "But when you ask, you must believe and not doubt, because the one who doubts is like a wave of the sea, blown and tossed by the wind." Having faith is removing all doubt from your mind. It is having a knowing within you that God will come through for you. I will share with you all in a chapter below how God led me through the process of breaking generational curses. That was a process of moving mountains from my life that were strong and deeply rooted. I can do all things through Christ who strengthens me (Philippians 4:13 NKJV). God has given you the strength and by His grace, you are able to overcome all obstacles set before you.

Faith Without Works

We can read in the Bible where a mountain (a giant Philistine) was taunting the children of Israel. The giant, Goliath, felt like because he was taller and bigger than everyone else, he had an advantage over the people. David had faith in God though. As he was tending to the sheep, he killed a bear and a lion that tried to take his sheep. God had prepared him for such a time as this. What seemed to be big and overbearing for others was not for David. He had enough faith in God to know that just how He delivered him from challenging the bear and the lion, that he would do the same when he accepted the challenge from Goliath, the giant Philistine. This is the same type of faith that we must have when faced with mountains. We can not shrink back, but we must believe that through Jesus Christ, we are victorious.

Sin is a mountain in the lives of many Christians. Many times we accept Jesus as Lord and Savior but do not know how to work our salvation out with fear and trembling (Philippians 2:12). The same sin that we came into the body of Christ with is the same sin we struggle with five years later. God desires that transformation come to our lives when we accept His son. We need to also accept and invite the Holy Spirit into our lives so that we may receive conviction when the desire to sin comes. We all are tempted by sin but through the grace of God, we are able to overcome. To receive a breakthrough in your life from sin, I suggest that you first believe that God will deliver you and that doubt is far from you. It is always a requirement for us to get before God and ask that He helps us with our weaknesses. But he said to me, "My grace is sufficient for you, for my power is made perfect in weakness. Therefore I will boast all the more gladly of my weaknesses, so that the power of Christ may rest upon me (2 Corinthians 12:9 ESV)."

You will overcome; not by your power, not by your might but by the Spirit of the living God (Zechariah 4:6). Read the Word of God because it will combat every lie and condemnation that the enemy tries to bring upon you. You will learn that God loves you and is rooting for you to surrender to Him for complete transformation. Your mindset is what will dictate whether you become free or you fall back into sin. Remember that a righteous man falls seven times but gets back

Faith Without Works

up again (Proverbs 24:16). None of us are perfect except Jesus but as we continue in God, He is working us to perfection. "Therefore you shall be perfect, just as your Father in heaven is perfect (Matthew 5:48)." I believe many people fall into sin because of the company they keep. If you have given your life to Christ, you can not continue to associate yourself with bad company. "Do not be misled: "Bad company corrupts good character (1 Corinthians 15:33 NIV)." So let's make a decision today what is more important to us.

I had many mountains in my life. I was a fornicator, adulterer, liar, drug addict, homeless, angry, bitter, and much more. These situations didn't move in my life until I surrendered to God. Many times when we come to Christ, we get caught up in trying to fix ourselves. With this mindset, we will fail because we are flesh. The spirit is willing but the flesh is weak (Matthew 26:41). I used to have this mindset at the beginning that I had to fix myself until I learned to rest in God and allow Him to do a work in me. This is all by faith.

CHAPTER 14

Faith Journey

I want to share my faith journey with you so that you may be encouraged in your faith journey with God. He is right alongside you keeping you, protecting you, and providing your every need. I have been placed on a journey where the Lord has built my faith. In the beginning, my faith was very minimal. I can admit, I didn't even know what faith really was. I heard the word being used and I even knew the Scripture that faith without works is dead. The Scriptures even give us the definition of faith in Hebrews 11:1, "Now faith is the substance of things hoped for, the evidence of things not seen." Does this mean that everything I hope for can happen?

I didn't even realize that believing in Jesus is having faith. We believe and stand for God whom we haven't seen and believe a book that is said to be inspired by Him (2 Timothy 3:16). This is great faith to place our lives in a hope that we do not have any physical ties to. Though you have not seen him, you love him; and even though you do not see him now, you believe in him and are filled with an inexpressible and glorious joy, for you are receiving the end result of your faith, the salvation of your souls (1 Peter 1:8-9 NIV).

My faith journey with God started in 2017. I was in a place of despair, brokenness, lack, and not knowing who I was. The God in whom I've never seen started tugging at my heart. He started to cause me to realize that there was more to me and life than what was currently going on. He started sending people to me randomly at my job to give me direction. I'll never forget the day that He sent a lady to tell me, "What if God tells you to quit your job?" I replied, "Then I would do it," even though at this current time I wasn't sure that I would. She responded, "God says quit your job." She said more things but this really stood out to me. At this time, I still had the mindset that I had to be perfect before I would be accepted by God. I used to believe that I had to make sure my life was lined up with the Word of God fully before I could go to church. See, I was hurt in the church. I do not want to blame anyone for the decisions I made but I truly loved my church and my pastor. Many times I would go to certain leaders and admit to them the wrong I had done. "Confess your faults one to another, and pray one for another, that ye may be healed. The effectual fervent prayer of a righteous man availeth much (James 5:16)."

Their response is what threw me off. "You should have done this and you should have done that," is what I was told. Yes, I know what I should have done but I didn't do it that way and I can't go back in time to fix it. My sins were also called out in front of the entire church. I do not mean like someone preaching from the pulpit and calling things out randomly or talking to you one on one but I'm talking about my name being called and the sin along with it. This really crushed my spirit and I started to believe that God was mean and didn't love me. Especially being that this was done at a time that I was praying to God to help me overcome this sin and the same week, it was called out in front of everyone.

Let's go back to that day that I received the prophetic word from the woman to quit my job. I continued on the job for about six more months. At this time, I was building a relationship with God. I was still shacking up with my boyfriend and smoking marijuana daily, but I knew God was calling me out of that. In October, I told my boyfriend that God was calling me to ministry and we had to get married or he would have to leave. He decided to marry me. We didn't wait at all. We got married within 1 or 2 weeks. I still had that marijuana addiction but just how God moved quickly for me to get married, He did the same for this addiction. I kept praying for God to remove that desire from me. In early November, the first week, the Lord took that taste away from me and I haven't looked back. My faith was being built in God. He had already shown Himself strong.

I was becoming on fire for God already. I wanted to get to know more about Him. I heard that fasting helps to hear God and be led by Him. I had never done this in my life, but whatever it took to have more of God who swept me from my sinful desires, I had to go deeper. I started doing fruits only fast and Daniel fast. I wanted it to be a sacrifice, so I did it around Thanksgiving. While my family was eating turkey and macaroni and cheese, I was eating vegetables and whole grain. I was praying even more. One day in prayer, the Lord told me that He called me to be a prophet. I was not even sure I was hearing God because this was all new to me. I was thinking, why would I call myself that though? I don't even know what it is or what they do. I just kept that word close to me and kept getting closer to God. Well, I was still working this job and more people were being sent to me from God. I was invited to a church but was pretty hesitant about going. I didn't attend until December 24, 2017. I didn't know what to expect based on the experiences I had over 13 years prior. This was not the same church but I didn't know anybody besides the woman who had invited me. My husband and I went and we received prayer. I was told on that day that God had called me to ministry and that He was birthing it out. What this meant, I really didn't know. I didn't go to this church regularly in the beginning but I made sure I prayed daily.

At the job that I was working, I was receiving lots of backlash even though they claim to have an open-door policy where you can tell management things that are bothering you. I had issues with coworkers not doing anything and all the workload being put on me. They would let people stand around and do nothing but ask me to come in at 4 am to get everything back to how it should be. When I expressed certain injustices, I was the one in the wrong. My hours started getting cut from 40 to 9 hours. I was distraught. I couldn't believe that after all the hard work I was putting in, they would do this to me. I cried out to God that day towards the end of January 2018. The Lord spoke to me so clearly, the clearest I have ever heard Him. He said, "Quit your job." Wow, I was hearing the same thing that was prophesied in the summer of 2017. I said, "God, today." He said, "Have integrity in everything you do. Put your two weeks notice in." Best believe that Satan also spoke. I heard him say "Do not be deceived."

See he will come to try to throw you off course and sound like an angel of light. But I laughed and proceeded to do what God had told me to do. I went on that job, went to HR, and put my two weeks notice in. It felt good even though I did not know what the future held for me. I didn't realize that everything that was happening during this time was called faith. It was the substance of things hoped for, the evidence of things not seen.

This was only the beginning of my journey because now that I no longer had a job, I had to trust God to supply all of my needs. After I quit this job, two months later my car was totaled. I was picking my daughter up from school when someone crashed into the driver's door of my car as I entered the parking lot. Now I am left with no car because I had no income to replace what I had lost. It seemed like things were getting worse and maybe I missed God but I had to use my faith and trust that what I heard was God even in those difficult times. Somehow God still made a way for me to be able to get around when I needed to and He also made sure that we were secure financially. I am not saying that I didn't have any struggles, but I can assure you that God always came through.

During my time of spiritual growth and my faith-building process, I learned many lessons. I went through the school of the Holy Spirit, where I had to learn the voice of God. I learned the way He speaks to me and was able to walk by faith and not by sight (2 Corinthians 5:7). I was able to learn not to look at my surroundings but to trust and believe the Word of God. Studying, meditating, reading, speaking, and praying the Word of God changed my life. My life went from rebellion to obedience. Totally obeying the voice of God will bring prosperity to your life. Believe in the Lord your God, so shall ye be established; believe his prophets, so shall ye prosper (2 Chronicles 20:20). As I continued to obey the voice of God, through dreams, visions, His true prophets, and through His still small voice (Holy Spirit), even though I was uncomfortable, my life began to shift. The Lord told me to do a 'Facebook Live' and talk about my addiction to marijuana. I stepped out, did the 'Facebook Live' and got invited to speak at a Boys & Girls Club. I was in such awe of God that He opened a door so quickly. This was my first time speaking in public, so I was nervous but the Holy Spirit gave me exactly what to say. By faith, I spoke what He told me and His spirit was very present as I did it. I am sure those that attended were blessed because the Lord knew exactly who would be there and who needed that message.

As I continued to grow in God, My faith increased more and more. When I was led by God through the many avenues He spoke to me personally, I overcame fear. Fear was a deep-rooted spirit within me that was generational. Many opportunities I could have taken in life, I declined due to having fear of the unknown. This fear gripped me and caused me to miss out on life. When I started noticing that having faith was the opposite of fear, my life shifted again. I would read in the Word that perfect love casts out fear because fear has torment. "There is no fear in love; but perfect love casteth out fear: because fear hath torment. He that feareth is not made perfect in love (1 John 4:18)." I would think to myself as I meditate on this Scripture and realize that God is perfect love. When we have perfect love, fear has to leave. As I meditated on the Word of God and got it deep within my heart, the way I used to think failed. I used to have dreams where the enemy was stronger than me and I would not be able to move or speak. As I built faith in God, I started having dreams of me putting a knife through the heart of demons. I also had an encounter with the spirit of fear in a dream. It appeared to me and tried to bind me but I spoke and said Psalm 23:4, "Yea, though I walk through the valley of the shadow of death, I will fear no evil: for thou art with me; thy rod and thy staff they comfort me." I had gotten that Word in my heart so fear could no longer bind me but it had to leave. "Ye are of God, little children, and have overcome them: because greater is he that is in you, than he that is in the world (1 John 4:4)."

CHAPTER 15

Breaking Generational Curses

Many of us are not seeing breakthroughs in our lives because we come from a family that operates in these practices. God may have revealed to you in a vision or dream that very practice that has held you up in your spiritual life and your physical life. God wants to set you free and break these demonic strongholds off of your life so that you and your family line may walk in total freedom.

I experienced this very thing. This is why I decided to write this section in this book so that you may receive total freedom from any practice your family may have participated in. When our family participated in the occult, they made covenants with demonic spirits to protect them, guide them, or it may even be an organization that they joined from generation to generation. There is now a door open in the spiritual realm that gives the enemy legal right to bring havoc into your life. They may have been ignorant to what they have actually done. I know from personal experiences within my family that the person they visited to get their palms read, tarot cards read, and receive potions and such were told that their gift came from God. These people may have deceived your family members into thinking that they are hearing and doing the work of God. Do not be deceived and ignorant of Satan's devices. My family opened the door to the demonic realm by joining freemasonry. My grandfather and other family members were a part of this and some still are.

When I went on my journey of healing and deliverance, I had a clear message from the Lord. I was in between sleep and awake. I heard the words "Eastern Star" very loud and clear. The Lord was giving me revelation as to the doors that were still open in my life due to my family's practices. I went online and found some renunciations that I could say to start breaking this from my life. The process to total freedom may take years, so I need you to be patient. If this is something that was in your family line for generations, it will not happen overnight. I'm letting you know because I do not want you to give up or think that God is not working on your behalf. God is going to teach you so much in this process and you will gain so much strength and authority over the enemy. I also went to deliverance sessions that were held at my church but to be honest, I received no breakthrough in those sessions. The deliverance minister kept praying and tried to find the root but the enemy would not leave. We were going at this for two hours and they were tired so I left still bound with generational curses over my life. But God was faithful enough to teach me how to get free. The Lord would show me through dreams and visions, things in the past that happened, which seemed to be hundreds of years prior. He would also allow me to get to the root so that I may intercede on behalf of my family line. After waking from these dreams, I would go into prayer breaking, binding, and rebuking the enemy's plans and loosing the plans of God according to what was shown.

As God continued to open my eyes in the night, I began to see breakthroughs in those dreams where it may have seemed that the enemy was winning prior, things started to shift where I was winning. Those strongholds began to break in the spiritual realm. I would also suggest that you add fasting because this really accelerated my sight and revelation to breaking the generational curses. The Lord also showed me in Scripture, principles of the spirit, and these were my foundational prayers along with the Holy Spirit leading me in the Courts of Heaven. The Lord allowed me to pray effective prayers that shut the mouth of the accuser. Then I heard a loud voice in heaven, saying, "Now the salvation, and the power, and the kingdom (dominion, reign) of our God, and the authority of His Christ have come;

for the accuser of our [believing] brothers and sisters has been thrown down [at last], he who accuses them and keeps bringing charges [of sinful behavior] against them before our God day and night (Revelation 12:10 AMP)."

Many people do not actually read the Word of God, so they do not know the authority they have in Christ. They do not understand that Jesus became the curse so that we may be free. "But Christ has rescued us from the curse pronounced by the law. When he was hung on the cross, he took upon himself the curse for our wrongdoing. For it is written in the Scriptures, "Cursed is everyone who is hung on a tree (Galatians 3:13 NLT)." This is why we now have the authority through Christ to break every curse that was pronounced over us due to our wrongdoings. We are not trapped but we are free in Christ.

To start your journey on healing and deliverance from occult practices whether it be from what you have done or your family, I would recommend you ask God what you need to renounce and that it may be pulled up from the root. I would google renunciation from occult practices.

There may be many pages to go through but do not skip them. Go through them and say them aloud with authority. Next, I would suggest you go through deliverance if possible at your church or somewhere that does deliverance. You need to get in the Word of God and find Scriptures that deal with your situation. Make those Scriptures the foundation for your prayers while you allow the Holy Spirit to lead you boldly to the throne of grace to receive mercy. Let us, therefore, come boldly to the throne of grace, that we may obtain mercy and find grace to help in time of need (Hebrews 4:16 NKJV).

RELEASING GENERATIONAL BLESSINGS

Now that we have renounced, repented, and interceded let's build our faith to start receiving blessings from the Lord. The Lord wants to release generational blessings that were held up due to the curses that were blocking them from flowing. "I will confirm my covenant with you and your descendants after you, from generation to generation. This is the everlasting covenant: I will always be your God and the God of your descendants after you (Genesis 17:7 NLT)." When we are obedient to God by following His Word, His Word will become living and active in our life. The promises that are written will become a reality for those that are walking uprightly before Him. Read Deuteronomy 28:1-14 to know some of the promises that God has in store for those that are willing and obedient. "If you are willing and obedient, you shall eat the good of the land (Isaiah 1:19 ESV)." Each day begin to decree and declare the will of God for your life according to the word of God.

I had a dream over a year ago and the Lord said to me, "Son of David." This is when I started my study on Jesus, David, and Solomon. The Holy Spirit gave me a revelation about generational blessings. I had been studying the books of Samuel. This book taught me the character of a true prophet and the life of King David. Since the Lord has been highlighting to me the wisdom, ability to build, and being able to finish it through Solomon, I wanted to go back and read on Solomon's dad and family line. The Lord promised Solomon to give him what He promised David as long as He obeyed Him (1 Kings 6:11-14).

As I was reading 1st and 2nd Samuel, I saw that God promised David to never leave Him like He left Saul. He always delivered David from His enemies and gave Him guidance. David always inquired of the Lord before He went into battle. The Lord also promised David to make his name great because David represented God in spirit and in truth. He was a true worshiper. Even when he messed up in life, he would get before God and worship. Worship is a lifestyle. When he got out of the will of God with Bathsheba, he had to get back in proper alignment with God. When we step out of the will of God, there are consequences. David's consequence for taking another man's wife and killing him was that his baby would not live and there would be confusion in his household. The same way he caused turmoil in someone else's life, the Lord allowed the same to happen to him and his family.

God did not allow the first child to live between Bathsheba and David but the second child,

Solomon, came with a promise. Since David was back in proper alignment with God, his seed is now able to receive the blessings. I believe God is saying, even if our family messed up and caused a curse to be on the bloodline, He is bringing you out. You are the bloodline breaker that will build for the kingdom of God and finish it. The promises of God are yes and amen. As long as we stay in proper alignment with God and keep His commandments, He will manifest those promises even back from our father. Yes, generational blessings. Are you ready to receive generational blessings that were held up because of the disobedience in your bloodline? I know I am. We must keep our hearts pure and know that God is going to release and fulfill every promise that He spoke.

Jesus came through David's bloodline. Your promises will manifest because King Jesus paid the price so that the curse may be broken from your family line. "Christ hath redeemed us from the curse of the law, being made a curse for us: for it is written, Cursed is every one that hangeth on a tree: That the blessing of Abraham might come on the Gentiles through Jesus Christ; that we might receive the promise of the Spirit through faith (Galatians 3:13-14)."

CHAPTER 16

The Just Shall Live By Faith

Everything that we believe in, do, and become in the Kingdom of God is by faith. Even though we do not see things or we see the opposite of the Word of God, it is our duty as Christians to have faith in the Word of God. We can not afford to waver and revert to witchcraft to make things happen faster in our lives. Always remember that God has the perfect timing for everything to manifest. He has it all planned out strategically to work into play at that appointed time. The ways of the Lord are not ours neither are His thoughts like ours. "For my thoughts are not your thoughts, neither are your ways my ways, saith the LORD. For as the heavens are higher than the earth, so are my ways higher than your ways, and my thoughts than your thoughts (Isaiah 55:8-9)." This is why we must live by faith.

What does "the just shall live by faith" mean? Well if we look in the Bible when Moses was told to go to Pharaoh and tell him to let his people go and Pharaoh wouldn't, Moses had to still have faith that what God said was coming to pass. When they were stuck between Pharaoh and His army and the Red Sea, Moses had to have faith that God would part the sea as he pointed his rod. Even when the Israelites were free in the wilderness with no food, Moses had to have faith that God would provide for the people. They had to live by faith. They went on a journey not knowing where they were going or what they had to endure but they believed the Word of the Lord and followed His plan.

The "just shall live by faith" means that you have surrendered to God. You believe the Word of God. You are walking based on the Word of God and not by what you see. You do not let anything cause your faith to waver. You trust God that He will provide for you. When it looks like everything has dried up, you use your mouth to declare the Word of the Lord. You wait on God for everything and you do not go ahead of Him.

CHAPTER 17

Faith Without Works

God wants His people to shift in their mindset. When we come to Christ, He does not want us to stay in the mode of just believing we are saved but to continue on in the process. There is a process after salvation where the Holy Spirit wants to cleanse us from our worldly mindsets. He wants to transform our minds as we read His word. God wants to get to our deep-rooted issues when we come into His presence. As we spend time with God, He will begin to pull back layers of sin, mess, disappointments, and every attachment that we received from this world. This is why having faith is good but without work, it's dead.

When we begin to step out in faith and allow God to do a work in us, we will be able to minister to others. God brings deliverance to us through our faith and works put together. Many people are bound because they think that just because they believe in Christ that they are free. Yes, believe the word of the Lord but the word also says to work out our salvation with fear and trembling. "Dear friends, you always followed my instructions when I was with you. And now that I am away, it is even more important. Work hard to show the results of your salvation, obeying God with deep reverence and fear (Philippians 2:12 NLT)."

I explained in the chapters above how I combined my faith with works and how God moved in my life. I didn't remain complacent with just being saved but I started to work towards my relationship with God. As I worked on knowing

God through His word, worship, prayer, dream, visions, and every area possible my life started lining up with His Word. We can not only read the Word but we must speak the Word too. We can not only speak the Word but we must do the word. "But don't just listen to God's word. You must do what it says. Otherwise, you are only fooling yourselves. For if you listen to the word and don't obey, it is like glancing at your face in a mirror. You see yourself, walk away, and forget what you look like. But if you look carefully into the perfect law that sets you free, and if you do what it says and don't forget what you heard, then God will bless you for doing it (James 1:22-25 NLT)."

Would you trust God if He told you to stop taking your medication if you have an illness? In 2015, I was diagnosed with diabetes. I was not serving God at this time, so I was so disappointed and felt like, yet another area of my life was being attacked. I was put on medication that I had to take twice per day to keep my sugar levels regulated. When I rededicated my life to Jesus, during prayer and worship in my intimate time with Him, He said, "Whose report do you believe?" I immediately knew He was referring to diabetes. That day I stopped taking my medication and my blood sugar levels remained normal. It was not until I was under attack spiritually, that they went back up. Even after the attack, the Lord told me again, "Stop taking your medicine." At first, I listened to Him and put the medicine away. I started checking my blood sugar and they were a little elevated. Instead of me trusting the report of the Lord, I started taking the medicine again. I did it for three days. On the third day, my sugar levels dropped so low, I became jittery and felt like I was going to pass out. Since that day, I have not taken the medication and I am fine. See, we must have faith and trust that what God tells us is the truth. We do not know what is ahead, but He does. We can not have wavering faith.

So then faith comes by hearing, and hearing by the word of God (Romans 10:17 NKJV). Now that you have heard the Word of the Lord and what He is requiring of the church, apply it to your lives. No more time to walk in emptiness, rebellion and in ignorance but come out of agreement with darkness. Step into His marvelous light that He has prepared for you before you were conceived in your mother's womb. We will no longer grieve the Spirit of God but we will allow Him to operate through our lives by using faith. We will trust God in every aspect of our lives. We will not lean to our own understanding, but we will acknowledge Him in all our ways and He will direct our paths (Proverbs 3:5-6).

About the Author

Kentia R. Middleton is a prophetic voice that God has raised up for such a time as this to expose the darkness in the Earth and the lies the enemy has told. She desires that all discover who they are in Christ. She has a heart for those that are less fortunate, rejected, abused, and misused. She wants to help many through her deliverance ministry.

After many struggles in life, Jesus came and captured Kentia's heart. She received deliverance, healing, and breakthrough from her many encounters with God. He mandated her to go forth and set the captives free by her incredible testimonies. She has a blog called 'More Than Enough,' where she tells her testimonies and releases prophetic words to warn and encourage the body of Christ. She has a ministry called Freedom in Christ Deliverance Ministries, where she desires to equip God's people with the necessary knowledge and wisdom needed to obtain a prosperous life. God wants to place every lost person on a path to finding out who they are. He wants His people to know His voice and follow Him. Her ministry will lead every person to Jesus and learn of His love, goodness, and mercy. It will also provide support for those in need, whether that be spiritual, mental, or financial.

She is married to Spencer and a mother to two children. She has a bachelor's degree in accounting with a minor in business. She is currently pursuing a master's degree in business management. She has a business called KRM Creative Designs, LLC where she creates logos, flyers, websites, and much more for ministries and businesses. She authors a book called More

Than Enough: Rejected by Man but Accepted by God. She is a member of Rain Fire Ministries International e-church. She has been mentored by Kimberly Moses for the past two years and serves in Kimberly Moses Ministries.

Kentia has a big vision that she is working diligently to complete.

Her blog website is http://www.morethanenough1.com

Ministry website is http://www.freedominchristdm.com

Business website is http://www.krmcreativedesigns.com

You may contact her at info@freedominchristdm.com

References

1. Merriam-Webster.com Dictionary, s.v. "astrology," accessed June 6, 2020, https://www.merriam-webster.com/dictionary/astrology.

2. Dictionary.com Dictionary, s.v. "sage," accessed June 6, 2020, https://www.dictionary.com/browse/sage

3. "Healing Crystals 101: Finding the Right One for You." n.d. Healthline. https://www.healthline.com/health/mental-health/guide-to-healing-crystals#1.

4. Dictionary.com Dictionary, s.v. "yoga," accessed June 6, 2020, https://www.merriam-webster.com/dictionary/yoga

5. Dictionary.com Dictionary, s.v. "ouija board," accessed June 6, 2020, https://www.dictionary.com/browse/ouija--board?s=t

6. Merriam-Webster.com Dictionary, s.v. "magic," accessed June 6, 2020, https://www.merriam-webster.com/dictionary/magic.

7. Merriam-Webster.com Dictionary, s.v. "black magic," accessed June 6, 2020, https://www.merriam-webster.com/dictionary/black%20magic.

Index

A

altar, 54, 56, 62
appointments, 52
astrology, 14
Astronomy, 14
atmosphere, 24, 28
authority, 3, 28, 47, 72, 96, 98

B

bless, 11, 47, 109

C

captives, 8, 113
child, 71, 101
Christ, 3, 68, 81–83, 98, 108
church, 3, 6–7, 48–49, 51–52, 55–56, 58, 60–62, 64–65, 76, 89, 99, 110
claim, 16, 41, 89
cleanse, 24, 38, 107
condemnation, 6, 82
confirmation, 49
control, 11, 33
conversation, 52
covenants, 20, 95
coworkers, 48, 89
crystals, 27–28
cults, 19, 21, 65
currency, 67
curse, 98–99, 102

D

darkness, 40, 44, 46, 112
deliverance, 99, 108, 113
disappointments, 108
disobedience, 102
doors, 35, 38, 96
dreams, 76, 94, 97

drunkenness, 43

E

enemy, 13, 28–29, 35, 38, 42, 72, 82, 95
energy, 27
episodes, 60, 62
everyday life, 15

F

faith, 1–2, 4, 48, 67–68, 71–73, 75, 78–81, 83, 85, 99, 104–6, 108, 110
faithfulness, 17
family, 20, 22, 42, 88, 94–95, 101–2
family members, 18, 95
faults, 53, 86
fear, 20–21, 93, 108
fear tactics, 21
flesh, 15–16
food, 61, 105
forgive, 13, 38
freedom, 3, 29
Freemasonry, 18
fruits, 21, 47

G

generational, 92
generations, 48, 96
God, 2–3, 5–8, 10–13, 19–24, 34, 41–44, 48–51, 58–59, 65–78, 80–83, 85–88, 90–91, 93–98, 100–102, 104–14
golds, 21, 28
grace, 13, 82, 99
gravitate, 15
guide, 34, 75, 95

H

healing, 29, 33, 113
hearts, 4, 11, 17, 46–47, 76, 102
heaven, 68, 75, 83, 97
Holy, 74
homes, 23–25, 37
horoscopes, 14–16
hurt, 45

I

intercessors, 60

J

Jesus, 16, 28–29, 41, 44, 72, 79, 83, 85, 112
journey, 46, 60, 66
joy, 8, 17, 27, 29, 47
judgment, 6, 44

K

kindness, 17, 47
kingdom, 44, 67–68, 104

L

legs, 36, 56–57
letters, 36
Leviticus, 24–25, 43
lifestyles, 10, 101
lion, 81
lips, 54
love, 13, 17, 20–21, 27, 44, 47, 68, 87, 92

M

magic, 40–42
maid, 71–72

manifest, 67, 72, 75, 102
manifestations, 5
married couple, 12
meditation, 31–33
mediums, 36
mentor, 7, 56
mindsets, 26, 48, 82
minister, 108
ministry, 87
mom, 59
mountain, 79–80
multicultural, 49
mustard, 79

N

net, 7, 15–16, 19, 24, 29, 34, 45, 63, 70, 82, 88, 96–97, 99

O

occult, 21, 95
occult practices, 98
organizations, 19–20, 22, 95
ouija boards, 36–38

P

parents, 10, 37
pastors, 7, 49, 55–56, 62
patience, 17, 47
peace, 1, 17, 24, 28–29, 34, 47
person, 5, 11–12, 24, 32–33, 60, 95
physical life, 94
physical postures, 31
power, 25, 28, 47–48, 82
pray, 12, 51, 86, 97
prayers, 11, 13, 22, 25, 35, 52, 75, 97, 99, 109
praying, 12, 51, 76, 96
process, 80, 96
profanity, 7, 54
profit, 1–2
promises, 71–72, 102
prophesy, 49, 51, 53
prophet, 62, 65
prophetic, 52–53
prophetic ministry, 52
prophetic words, 49, 52, 113
prosperous life, 113
protection, 27, 29, 42, 44
purge, 29, 48
purify, 25

R

rebellion, 20, 110
relief, 56, 61, 64
Religion, 5, 7
religious spirit, 5
Renounce, 44
repent, 3, 17, 22, 25, 29, 35, 38, 44–45
revelation, 48, 65, 96–97
righteous, 82, 86
righteousness, 2, 8, 73

S

salvation, 12, 97, 108
sheep, 81
sin, 25, 81–82, 86–87, 108
society, 37, 40–41
soul, 21–22, 46, 85
spirits, 2, 6, 15, 17, 20–21, 24, 32–33, 37, 43, 46, 48, 50, 53, 66–67, 97
spiritual growth, 6
spiritual life, 94
spouse, 12
stars, 14–15

strength, 73, 96
sugar levels, 109

T

territories, 38, 47
tongues, 64, 75–76
torment, 21, 29
traditions, 5, 23
trees, 8, 98, 102

V

victory, 38, 64
visions, 94, 97, 109, 114
voice, 91, 97

W

warfare, 56, 58, 71
wind, 34, 72
wisdom, 70–71, 113
witchcraft, 11–12, 40–42, 104
witches, 41–43, 65
words, 3, 6, 11, 16–17, 29, 34–36, 46, 52, 77, 100, 107, 109

worship, 23, 109

Z

zodiac signs, 14–16